T0209070

HOW TO ENHANCE YOUR MEDICAL ACADEMIC PORTFOLIO

A GUIDE FOR DOCTORS IN TRAINING

MOUSTAFA MANSOUR
Surgical Excellence Clinic Limited

SHAHAB and SHAHIN HAJIBANDEH

authorHOUSE®

AuthorHouse™ UK
1663 Liberty Drive
Bloomington, IN 47403 USA
www.authorhouse.co.uk
Phone: UK TFN: 0800 0148641 (Toll Free inside the UK)
*   UK Local: 02036 956322 (+44 20 3695 6322 from outside the UK)*

Published by AuthorHouse   08/16/2021

ISBN: 978-1-6655-8957-4 (sc)
ISBN: 978-1-6655-8958-1 (e)

Moustafa Mansour, MB BCH, FHEA, FRCS (General Surgery)
Consultant Upper Gastro Intestinal and Laparoscopic Surgeon
Manchester University Foundation Trust
Greater Manchester, United Kingdom
Fellow of the Higher Education Academy of the United Kingdom
Fellow of the Royal College of Physicians and Surgeons of Glasgow

Shahab Hajibandeh, MBChB, MRCS
Member of the Royal College of Surgeons
Specialist Registrar in General Surgery
Wales Deanery, United Kingdom

Shahin Hajibandeh, MBChB, MRCS
Member of the Royal College of Surgeons
Specialist Registrar in General Surgery
West Midlands Deanery, United Kingdom

PREFACE

Successful progression through medical education and training in the United Kingdom and equivalent health systems is invariably dependent on various academic achievements. The significance of academic achievements is highlighted when medical students start approaching their final year of undergraduate education. At such a stage, medical students are expected to start applying for foundation training posts. Such significance is further highlighted towards the end of the foundation programme when trainees start applying for core and / or specialty training. Others will be seeking various fellowship programmes.

The significance of achieving a high academic profile becomes crucial year by year until trainees are awarded the certificate of completion of training, known as the CCT in the United Kingdom. While the current postgraduate medical and surgical training programmes allow trainees to develop clinical knowledge and skills required for progression to higher levels of training, it is recognised that such training programmes do not objectively guide current trainees on how to enhance their medical academic portfolios.

The majority of trainees, irrespective of their stage of

training, are constantly looking for ways to improve and enhance their medical academic portfolios. Such desire to become academically active is expected to continue beyond the initial stages of training and throughout years of independent practice. Several trainees who are academically active throughout their training continue to contribute to research, publications, and medical innovation after being appointed as consultants and independent practitioners.

How to Enhance Your Medical Academic Portfolio aims to serve as a systematic guide for medical students and doctors in training on how to enhance their medical academic portfolios. The authors of this book have extensive experience in designing research, leading on evidence synthesis, and working on quality improvement projects that have resulted in several publications in international peer-reviewed journals, as well as numerous presentations at national and international conferences and scientific forums.

They have experienced and witnessed different stages of undergraduate and postgraduate medical training in the United Kingdom and overseas. They are fully aware of the academic requirements for progression through higher levels of training. Such experience would make this book a potentially remarkable tool for doctors in training in the United Kingdom and for those overseas graduates who aim to pursue their postgraduate training and career progression in the United Kingdom and / or other countries with equivalent health care systems.

It is worth noting that this book is not aimed at describing how to write an academic paper or how to secure a training post. It is predominantly aimed at giving medical graduates and doctors in training the chance to enhance their medical academic portfolios and deal with the challenges and requirements of career progression in a simple, systematic, and clear way using a well-recognised methodological approach.

This book, in addition to providing a systematic approach to choosing a specialty appropriate to trainees' skills and capabilities, also provides advice in relation to different skills required for various specialties and subspecialties. It also provides invaluable information in relation to non-technical skills that are rarely mentioned in similar books tackling academic challenges.

There will be detailed discussion about challenges that have recently been encountered by doctors in training, including the Covid-19 pandemic challenges, and the impact of such challenges on achieving the academic objectives that doctors in training are aspiring to. It will also address measures that can help in tackling such challenges in a pragmatic and systematic way.

We are confident that *How to Enhance Your Medical Academic Portfolio* provides the necessary information that will guide medical students and doctors in training throughout their medical education and training journey. It will also allow them to utilise certain tested and proven methods to achieve their career aspirations in parallel to achieving a well-balanced lifestyle, which is crucial to their success.

CONTENTS

CHAPTER 1

Domains of Academic Portfolio

Medical academic portfolios consist of different domains on which trainees should focus. All domains are important and contribute equally to the trainee's academic portfolio. Taking into account a trainee's clinical commitments and limited time available for additional activities, it is recognised that not all domains will be achievable by all trainees. It is therefore crucial to be realistic and pragmatic and to identify the domains that are achievable by each trainee in a timely manner.

What are the domains of an academic portfolio?

An academic portfolio includes the following domains:

- research and publications
- audits and quality improvement projects
- presentations
- courses and exams
- teaching
- leadership and management

- awards and prizes
- additional qualifications

In order to prioritise the foregoing areas for trainees who assumedly have no academic achievements, it is advisable to assess which domains can be achieved *prospectively and in a timely manner.* It is crucial to seek continuous guidance from senior colleagues and supervisors throughout this process as it is not uncommon to deviate from the main aim of a certain domain or to lose enthusiasm when setting a non-achievable academic target.

Research and publications

Participating in a research project leading to publications in peer-reviewed journals is feasible and achievable for all trainees irrespective of their stage of training. This is providing that the trainee participates in a relevant project with appropriate study design and achievable end points. Moreover, this domain will invariably facilitate achievement of other domains, including Presentations and Leadership and Management. (Please refer to Chapter 2: Research and Publications.)

Audits and quality improvement projects

Participating in clinical audits and quality improvement projects is feasible and is easily achievable by a trainee. This domain invariably facilitates achievement of two other domains, namely Presentations and Leadership and Management. (Please refer to Chapter 3: Audits and Quality Improvement Projects.)

Presentations

After completion of a research or quality improvement project, results may be presented by the trainee at local, national, and international meetings and conferences. Oral and/or poster presentations would invariably enhance the trainee's portfolio. (Please refer to Chapter 4: Presentations.)

Courses and exams

Participation in relevant core and speciality training courses and completion of relevant exams are easily deliverable and achievable targets. This domain can be achieved by doctors in training in a timely manner providing that adequate time and resources are allocated during prospective planning. (Please refer to Chapter 5: Courses and Exams.)

Teaching

Participation in various teaching activities at local and regional levels is feasible and achievable by all trainees, irrespective of their stage of training. This domain invariably facilitates achievement of another domain, namely Leadership and Management. (Please refer to Chapter 6: Teaching.)

Leadership and management

Demonstration of leadership and management skills at local, regional, and potentially national levels is feasible and achievable by almost all trainees. This domain eventually can be supported by other domains, mentioned above. (Please refer to Chapter 7: Leadership and Management.)

Awards and prizes

Earning an academic award or prize cannot be fully influenced or controlled by the individual trainee. It is well recognised that getting involved in more research projects, delivering more presentations, and achieving high scores in various exams increases the chance of being nominated for an award or prize. There is no guarantee that this domain can be achieved in a timely manner. However, there are steps that trainees may take to increase their chances of being nominated for an award. (Please refer to Chapter 8: Prizes, Awards, Additional Qualifications.)

Additional qualifications

Some medical students are awarded additional qualifications prior to or during their study for their primary medical degree. Some trainees also take time out of their training programmes at different stages of their training to gain additional qualifications. Gaining additional qualifications is feasible and has a significant impact on trainees' academic portfolios. However, it is recognised that unless the individual has already been awarded an additional qualification prior to applying for further training programmes, this domain cannot be achieved *in a timely manner* prior to such applications.

As discussed above, all the aforementioned domains except Awards and Prizes and Additional Qualifications can be achieved prospectively and in a timely manner. Additionally, achievement of one domain may invariably facilitate achievement of others. It is therefore crucial to understand how different domains are integrated and interlinked with each other.

Figure 1.1 demonstrates how the foregoing domains are related.

In the following chapters of *How to Enhance Your Medical Academic Portfolio*, each domain will be discussed in detail, and the diagram presented in Figure 1.1 will be broken down and discussed further. The order of the following chapters has been selected based on the priorities of a trainee who is assumed to have had no academic achievements so far. This reference book will invariably guide doctors in training with limited or no previous academic experience so they may achieve their academic goals in the increasingly competitive field of postgraduate medical and surgical training and education.

Figure 1.1 **Relationship between domains of academic portfolios**

Summary

- All the aforementioned domains contribute equally to trainees' academic portfolios.

- Not every single domain mentioned above is achievable by all trainees.

- All domains except Awards and Prizes and Additional Qualifications can be achieved in a timely manner.

- Achievement of one domain may invariably facilitate achievement of other domains.

CHAPTER 2

Research and Publications

Research is defined as a systematic investigation into certain materials and sources in order to establish facts and reach new conclusions. Involvement in research projects is crucial for medical and surgical trainees in order to be able to progress through the different stages of their training. The majority of trainees consider this domain as their weak point, and interestingly, this presumed weakness exists even at higher levels of training and beyond.

What makes most trainees reluctant to be involved in research is a fear of statistics. Unfortunate exposure to dry and solid statistical definitions and formulas without education on practical aspects of statistics in medical schools or during early years of training may explain such fear.

Nevertheless, it is important to recognise that clinicians are not expected to be professional statisticians. In fact, the understanding of practical aspects and the interpretation of basic statistics is all that is required in the majority of cases. A fear of statistics should never be a barrier to getting involved in various research projects.

Completing research projects could be achievable in a clinical setting as well as in a laboratory or a research-oriented placement depending on the nature of the research project and the clinical relevance. Clinically oriented research projects tend to be more achievable in a hospital setting, where interaction with patients and their investigations, including clinical outcomes, play a vital role in achieving the above-mentioned sought after results.

Some trainees would prefer to take a break from their clinically oriented hospital placements to focus more on laboratory-based nonclinical research projects. This remains a valid approach. However, it should be taken into account that laboratory-based nonclinical research projects may take a longer time to complete compared with clinical projects, and many may not be achievable in a timely manner.

This chapter of *How to Enhance Your Medical Academic Portfolio* describes the most efficient and practical approach to involvement in research projects which could potentially lead to recognisable publications.

What is expected of a trainee?

Each trainee is expected to demonstrate that he or she has been the author of significant peer-reviewed, PubMed-cited original research publications. This statement is clarified below:

- **Significant authorship**
  This refers to first or co-first authorship of an original research publication. Although significant authorship is a requirement to achieve the highest score for this domain, co-authorship is acceptable and also scores high.

- **Peer-reviewed**
  This refers to a manuscript that has been sent to one or more independent reviewers prior to acceptance for publication. Such reviewers would have reviewed and validated the manuscript and its contents in advance.

- **PubMed-cited**
  This refers to a publication which is cited in PubMed with a unique PubMed ID reference number.

- **Original research publication**
  This refers to published basic scientific or clinical research projects, as well as systematic reviews and meta-analyses.

What are different types of study designs?

There are different types of study designs in which a trainee can participate in or to which he or she can contribute. These include the following:

- systematic reviews and meta-analyses
- randomised controlled trials

- cohort studies (retrospective or prospective)
- case-control studies
- cross-sectional studies
- case series and case reports
- editorials and expert opinions

What are the most appropriate study designs for a trainee to participate in?

In order to select an appropriate study design as a research project, it is crucial to take into account the following factors:

- *Time and resources required to complete the project*
- *Level of evidence the research would provide.*

Figure 2.1 demonstrates the hierarchy of evidence based on each study design.

Systematic review and meta-analysis

This study design provides the highest level of evidence in literature and is considered as original research. A systematic review attempts to gather all research and available evidence on a certain topic through using well defined, systematic methodology aiming at obtaining answers to certain queries. A meta-analysis is defined as the process of dissecting and analysing available data and combining available results of similar studies and research projects. The project can be completed by trainees in a timely manner irrespective of the stage of their training. Trainees are therefore strongly recommended to conduct systematic reviews and meta-analyses at early stages of their training.

Randomised controlled trial

A randomised controlled trial is a type of scientific experiment in which subjects are randomly assigned to either the experimental group or the control group. Such trials aim to reduce bias when assessing or testing the efficacy of certain new treatments or interventions. This study design provides a high level of evidence in literature and is considered as original research. However, conducting a randomised controlled trial is expensive, time-consuming, and can be challenging. It is worth noting that the trainee will unlikely be able to complete randomised control trial projects in a timely manner. Participating in randomised controlled trials at early stages of training is therefore not always recommended for enhancing medical academic portfolios.

Cohort study

A cohort study is generally defined as a longitudinal study where researchers and investigators identify individuals or groups at a certain point in time when the outcome of interest is not readily available. Researchers then follow such individuals or groups over a period of time. Cohort studies usually recruit participants who share certain characteristics including those who live in a certain geographic areas, those who work in a certain occupation or those who have a common underlying health condition. This study design provides a moderate level of evidence in literature and is considered as original research. Conducting a cohort study is less challenging and less expensive than conducting randomised controlled trials, but it may have its own challenges and constraints. Retrospective cohort studies are easier to conduct than prospective cohort studies. The project should be selected very carefully by trainees so that it can be completed in a timely manner. Retrospective cohort studies are therefore recommended for trainees to participate in at early stages of their training.

Case-control study

Case control studies ideally compare two groups; one group of people or individuals with a certain condition or disease and another similar group who do not have or share the underlying condition or disease to be studied. This study design provides a moderate level of evidence in literature and is considered as original research. Conducting a case-control study is similar to conducting a retrospective cohort study, and if selected carefully, it can be completed in a timely manner by a trainee. Case-control studies are as recommended as retrospective cohort studies for trainees to participate in at early stages of their training.

Cross-sectional study

This study design provides a moderate level of evidence in literature and is considered as original research. Conducting a cross-sectional study is less challenging than conducting other observational studies. It requires access to a large sample size, but the study can be completed in a timely manner by a trainee. Cross-sectional studies are as recommended as retrospective cohort studies for trainees to participate in at early stages of their training. Authors advise to engage in designing and conducting cross-sectional studies at early stages of training.

Case series and case report

A case series is a study that tracks subjects with a known exposure or underlying pathology and examines their medical files and available information aiming to study exposure and outcomes. Case series may be consecutive or non-consecutive. A case report on the other hand, is a detailed report outlining presentation, investigations, diagnosis and management of an individual patient whose condition is thought to be of interest to the wider medical community. Case series and case reports provide a low level of evidence in literature and may potentially be considered as original research. They are very easy to conduct and can be completed in a timely manner. Case series and case reports do not score high in the publication domain, and some specialties do not actually consider them as original research. Despite the importance of case series and case reports, they are not routinely recommended to trainees for enhancing their academic portfolios.

Editorials and expert opinions

Editorials and expert opinions are not considered as original research and are not recommended to trainees for enhancing their academic portfolio.

Figure 2.1 **Hierarchy of evidence based on each study design**

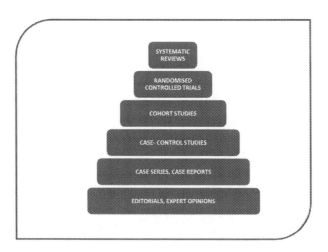

A trainee should aim at designing, leading and participating in as many projects as possible in the shortest time period so that the requirements by the relevant specialties are met in a timely manner. Among the study designs discussed above, systematic reviews and meta-analyses are the most recommended study designs for trainees. Retrospective cohort studies, case-control studies, and/or cross-sectional studies are the second-most recommended study designs for trainees. In order to develop the skills required for conducting systematic reviews and meta-analyses, it is recommended that trainees attend relevant courses and workshops enabling them to complete their projects independently.

What other domains are affected by this domain?

Involvement in research projects contributes to other domains of an academic portfolio. Trainees should submit the abstracts of their projects to regional, national, and/or international conferences and forums for presentation purposes. Trainees who take part in research projects as lead authors can use their collaboration as evidence for their leadership and management. **Figure 2.2** demonstrates the relationship between research and the other domains of academic portfolio.

Figure 2.2 Relationship between research and other domains

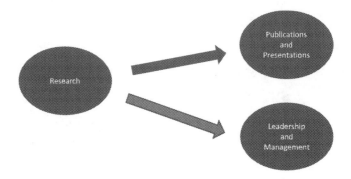

Summary

- Systematic reviews and meta-analyses are the most recommended study designs for trainees to participate in and lead on.

- Retrospective cohort, case-control, and cross-sectional studies are the second-most recommended study designs for trainees to participate in.

- Involvement in research projects will also contribute to the Presentations domain and the Leadership and Management domain of a trainee's portfolio.

CHAPTER 3

Audits and Quality Improvement Projects

A clinical audit is defined as a quality improvement process/project that aims at improving patient care and outcomes through systematic review of a service or care given against explicit criteria followed by implementation of change or changes if needed. Trainees are frequently offered involvement in audit projects by their current department or their supervisors. Most trainees, however, do not achieve the maximum scores for this domain. This highlights the fact that trainees should be very selective and careful when choosing a clinical audit/project to work on, with a clear audit protocol and project proposal associated with expected clear achievable outcomes.

This chapter describes the most efficient approach to involvement in audit and quality improvement projects.

What is expected of a trainee?

Trainees are expected to demonstrate that they have been involved in **designing**, **data collection**, **data**

analysis, and **presentation** of an audit project. If trainees demonstrate that they have completed the whole audit cycle, they are more likely to achieve the maximum scores for this domain.

Most audit projects completed by trainees do not meet the foregoing requirements. This is because of the fact that many trainees only take part in the data collection stage of such projects, which are usually led by others. Despite getting involved in several audit projects, trainees may never complete a full audit cycle.

Doctors in training are reminded that closing an audit loop or cycle is crucial in demonstrating the ability to identify the shortfall or deficiency in a service or practice. This will also demonstrate the ability to work on rectifying such deficiencies, then reassessing the impact of any suggested changes. Participating in at least one quality improvement project per year is mandatory for medical and surgical training career progression within the United Kingdom. It is strongly recommended that trainees initiate and lead on their own audit projects so they can demonstrate that they have been involved in all stages of the audit cycle.

How to initiate and complete a clinical audit project independently?

The steps required for completion of a clinical audit are described as follows:

Identifying a clinical problem or issue

This step involves careful observation of clinical practice in a specific clinical setting to identify deviation from a recognised standard clinical practice. There is a wide range of clinical practice issues that can be selected for clinical audit purposes. One might choose a simple issue such as poor quality of documentation during a ward round or a more complex issue such as high conversion rate to open surgery in patients undergoing laparoscopic cholecystectomy in a surgical department.

Setting measurable criteria and standards

This step involves defining how the identified issue is going to be measured (criterion) and determining the target that the audit aims to achieve for each measure (standard). If the identified issue is poor quality of documentation in ward rounds, one criterion to be audited could be documentation of patients' vital signs during ward rounds. The target standard for this criterion could be set at 100 per cent. This estimates that patients' vital signs are expected to be documented for all patients during ward rounds. Trainees may use specific local or national guidelines, if applicable, as a reference for setting criteria and standards.

Registering the audit with the clinical governance and audit department

Once a trainee identifies a clinical issue and sets appropriate criteria and standards, he or she should complete the audit registration form and submit it to the clinical governance and audit department. Trainees should specify themselves as leads for their audits and should select one consultant as supervisor in order to be able to register the audit. Once the audit project is registered, the clinical governance and audit department will formally issue an audit registration number specific to this project.

Identifying eligible population

Trainees should identify an eligible population for their audit project. The clinical governance and audit department may help trainees to identify the eligible population for their project if the audit is retrospective. On the other hand, the eligible population may be identified by trainees prospectively.

For example, in an audit of poor quality of documentation in ward rounds, the eligible population would be all patients who are currently admitted as inpatients in a respiratory or a surgical ward. The list of patients can be simply obtained from the ward clerk or ward sister in charge.

As another example, in the audit of high rates of conversion from laparoscopic to open surgery in patients undergoing laparoscopic cholecystectomy, the eligible population would be all patients undergoing laparoscopic cholecystectomy during a particular period within a unit/department. The list of patients can be obtained from the clinical governance and audit department as stated above.

Collecting data

Collecting data involves the creation of a data collection pro forma agreed with the audit lead, all participants, and the supervising consultant. Data collection pro forma helps trainees to collect data systematically and objectively. It is crucial to ensure that all relevant data are adequately captured at this stage. This will then ensure a smooth and trouble free data analysis stage. It is worth noting that any missing data on the pro forma will eventually lead to potential delays in completing the audit.

Analysing data

This step includes analysis of the collected data using simple descriptive statistics. The aim of analysis is to determine whether the target standard for each criterion has been achieved or not. For example, in the audit of poor quality of documentation in ward rounds, if the vital signs have been documented in 100 per cent of cases, then the target standard is considered to have been achieved for this criterion. If the documentation rate is less than 100 per cent, then the target standard is considered not to have been achieved, hence implementation of change would be warranted.

Implementing change/s

This step involves identifying a solution or a rectifying measure that can be applied in practice to improve the performance of or compliance with a certain standard criterion. This is a well-recognised step when target standards have not been achieved or met during baseline auditing. For example, in the audit of poor quality of documentation in ward rounds, if documentation of patients' vital signs has been substandard in the baseline audit, then a simple solution would be to include a checklist in ward round sheets to alert clinicians to document the vital signs accurately.

Re-auditing

This step involves repeating the audit after implementing the recommended changes. This aims at ensuring that target standards have been achieved. This process should ideally continue until the target standards are achieved for all criteria—and once achieved, the audit cycle can then be closed. In order to close an audit cycle, several re-audits might be required.

Presenting results

This step involves presentation of the audit results at clinical governance and audit meetings. On completion of the audit, an audit report and presentation should be submitted to the clinical governance and audit department. A certificate of completion will then be issued for the trainee. The certificate should specify the role of the trainee in relation to design, data collection, data analysis, and presentation of audit results.

What other domains are influenced by this domain?

Participation in various audit projects significantly contributes to other domains of the academic portfolio.

Depending on the scope and quality of the audit, the results may also be submitted for presentation at regional, national, and/or international meetings and conferences. The report of a full audit cycle may be submitted to relevant journals to be considered for publication.

Trainees who take part in audit projects as leads can use this participation as evidence of their leadership skills.

Figure 3.1 demonstrates the relationship between audit and quality improvement projects and the other domains of academic portfolios.

Figure 3.1 Relationship between audit and quality improvement projects and other domains

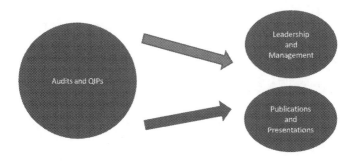

Summary

- It is strongly recommended that trainees initiate and lead their own audit projects at early stages of their training.

- Trainees are expected to be involved in designing, data collection, data analysis, and presentation of results of audit projects.

- Involvement in audit and quality improvement projects will invariably contribute to The Presentations domain and the Leadership and Management domain of a trainee's portfolio.

CHAPTER 4

Presentations

Presenting research projects at national and/or international meetings and conferences contributes significantly to a trainee's academic portfolio. Involvement in research or quality improvement projects provides the required material and associated data for various presentations at conferences, forums, and meetings.

This chapter describes the most efficient approach to improving the Presentations domain of academic portfolios.

Different types of presentations

Selected abstracts at meetings and/or conferences may be presented as the following:

- **Oral presentations**
  Presenters are expected to deliver a five-to-ten-minute talk on their projects in front of an audience. This is usually followed by a few minutes of questions and answers. During this session, audience members ask several

questions related to the project including methodology and outcomes, and the presenter is expected to respond to such queries. This significantly enhances the trainee's ability to communicate effectively and to deal with pressure created from being an oral presenter in front of an audience at such early stages of his or her training.

- **Poster presentations**
  Presenters are expected to prepare a paper or an electronic poster which is displayed at poster sessions at various conferences and meetings. Presenters are encouraged to remain in the area to answer any queries related to the poster. Again, this significantly enhances the trainee's ability to communicate effectively and to deal with pressure at such early stages of his or her training. Paper posters have been the tradition over many years; however, there has been a recent shift to electronic posters over the last few years.

What is expected of a trainee?

Trainees are expected to demonstrate that they have delivered several presentations at regional, national, and international meetings or conferences. The following points should be considered:

- Oral presentations are considered more valuable than poster presentations.
- National and international presentations are considered more valuable than regional presentations.
- The same abstract may be submitted to different regional, national, and/or international meetings or conferences depending on the terms and policies of relevant conferences and events. Trainees are always encouraged to check such terms in advance prior to submission.

Steps required for a successful presentation

The trainee should:

- Prepare an abstract after completion of a research or quality improvement project.
- Identify the most appropriate meetings or conferences which are nationally or internationally recognised. Such events should be relevant to the trainee's specialty area of interest.
- Submit the already prepared abstract to the identified conference or meeting. The abstract should be prepared according to the instructions and criteria provided by the conference organisers.

- Register for the conference or meeting once the abstract is accepted, then subsequently prepare the oral or poster presentation according to instructions provided by conference or meeting organisers.
- Attend the conference or meeting and subsequently deliver the presentation as previously scheduled.
- Collect a conference programme attendance certificate as well as a presentation certificate.
- Keep a record of such certificates as proof of presentation and attendance.

It is vital that trainees maintain the cycle of research, audit, and presentation. As discussed before, the completed research and audit projects provide the required material for presentations and publications.

Once a project is completed, trainees should aim to start a new project so they may achieve the required number of publications and presentations for their academic portfolios in a timely manner.

What other domains are influenced by this domain?

Most national and international conferences publish the abstracts in peer-reviewed journals as a supplementary issue. The published abstracts can also be used as evidence of presentation and may be listed separately in portfolios as an abstract publication.

Figure 4.1 demonstrates the relationship between presentations and other domains of an academic portfolio.

It is worth noting that presenting more projects at conferences, forums, and meetings increases the likelihood of winning prizes and/or awards. Such recognition is significantly important for trainees' academic portfolios.

Figure 4.1 Relationship between presentations and other domains

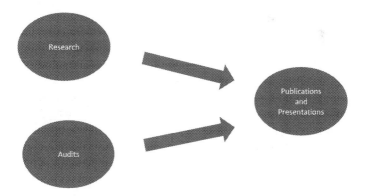

Summary

- Active involvement in research and quality improvement projects provides the required material for presentations at conferences and meetings.

- Oral presentations are generally considered more valuable than poster presentations.

- International and national presentations are again generally considered more valuable than regional ones.

- Presenting more projects at conferences and meetings increases the likelihood of winning prizes and/or awards.

CHAPTER 5

Courses and Exams

Attending appropriate continuing professional development (CPD) courses and completing appropriate exams is crucial for trainees' career progression. Interestingly, almost all trainees achieve high scores in this domain as they are already aware of such requirements far in advance.

Considering the foregoing fact, scoring low in this domain will inevitably result in a significant disadvantage for trainees. It is therefore strongly recommended that trainees identify essential requirements relevant to their specialty areas of interest as early as possible and that they plan to achieve such requirements and competencies by the respective deadlines.

It is always recommended that a trainee checks with his or her clinical and educational supervisors prior to booking exams and educational courses in order to ensure relevance of such exams and courses to his/her career progression.

While recognising that some exams and courses might

be mandatory in the trainee's curriculum, supervisors will also ensure that the trainee is ready to participate in such activities and will provide advice on any top-up training required prior to such engagement.

What other domains are affected by this domain?

Attending appropriate courses related to teaching skills and techniques, as well as leadership and management skills courses, not only helps to develop such required skills but also contributes significantly to the relevant domains.

Figure 5.1 demonstrates the relationship between courses and other domains of the academic portfolio.

Figure 5.1 Relationship between courses and other domains

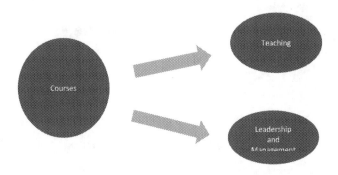

Summary

- The Courses and Exams domain is the most achievable domain by a trainee in a timely manner.

- The majority of trainees achieve the highest scores for this domain in a timely manner.

- Scoring low in this domain will inevitably result in a significant disadvantage for trainees.

- CPD courses and specialty-related exams are included as part of trainees' training curriculum and vary across different specialties.

CHAPTER 6

Teaching

Active involvement in teaching is crucial to all stages of medical career progression. All trainees, irrespective of their stage of training, are expected to deliver regular teaching sessions for their peers and junior colleagues. Teaching experience and commitments contribute significantly to trainees' academic portfolios.

This chapter describes some of the most efficient approaches to improving the Teaching domain of academic portfolios.

What are different types of teaching activities?

Different types of teaching activities include the following:

- ward-based clinical teaching
- small group tutorials and/or workshops
- delivery of lectures
- development and delivery of lecture series

- leading and development of courses and curricula
- attending courses on teaching techniques/skills

What is expected of a trainee?

Trainees are expected to demonstrate evidence of regular teaching commitments as well as evidence of validated feedback related to such commitments and activities.

Considering the wide range of teaching activities available to trainees, it is crucial to identify activities that can result in achievement of the maximum possible score in this domain.

Most appropriate teaching activities for a trainee

Ward-based clinical teaching

Almost all clinicians with various seniorities should regularly provide ward-based clinical teaching for their junior colleagues and medical students. It is important for trainees to participate in ward-based and bed side clinical teaching for training and educational purposes. Trainees and clinical teachers are advised to keep a record of their commitment and relevant feedback related to such activities. It is worth mentioning that ward-based clinical teaching on its own does not contribute significantly to enhancing trainees' academic portfolios. Trainees should not rely solely on this type of teaching activity.

Small group tutorials and workshops

These teaching activities, useful for developing and maintaining appropriate teaching skills, demonstrate a good basis for teaching commitments. Trainees are reminded to participate in these activities on a regular basis. They are again advised to keep a record of their commitment and relevant feedback from small group tutorials and workshops. Similar to regular ward-based clinical teaching, small group tutorials and workshops on their own do not contribute significantly to trainees' academic portfolios. As stated above, trainees should not rely solely on this type of teaching activity.

Delivery of lectures

Delivering lectures on a regular basis contributes significantly to a trainee's academic portfolio. Trainees are advised to collaborate closely with the undergraduate and postgraduate director of medical education at their base hospital/institution to deliver regular lectures at different training programmes. Moreover, trainees should receive a validated certificate for and feedback from any lectures they deliver as evidence that can be provided if and when required.

Development and delivery of lecture series

This is considered one of the most valued teaching activities that a trainee can participate in. It involves the creation of a teaching programme comprised of a series of lectures delivered by the trainee or other lectures for specific groups of trainees and medical students. This teaching programme can be organised at the local and/or regional level. The director of undergraduate or postgraduate medical education and his or her administrator teams should be approached by trainees for approval and dissemination of the programme and associated activities. This will ensure that appropriate planning and resource allocation are put in place for such activities in advance. Creation and delivery of lecture series will result in achievement of maximum scores in the Teaching domain of academic portfolios.

Leading and development of courses and curricula

This is also considered to be one of the most valued teaching activities a trainee could participate in. It involves development of a clinical or nonclinical course for a specific group of trainees. The course may be organised at the local, regional, or even national level. The trainee should design a programme for the proposed course, demonstrate the evidence of competency for delivering the course, and specify a group of delegates and candidates who could benefit from such a course or activity.

It is again recommended for the programme to be submitted to the director of undergraduate or postgraduate medical education and his or her administrator teams for approval and to plan for required resources. Leading and development of a course or curriculum also results in achievement of the maximum score in the Teaching domain of academic portfolios.

Attending courses on teaching techniques/skills

Attending courses such as training the trainers or acting as an instructor for clinical courses is essential for development of teaching skills and contributes to the trainee's academic portfolio. Despite their importance, these courses should not be considered as the sole teaching activity and should be used in parallel with other activities.

What other domains are influenced by this domain?

Involvement in teaching activities contributes to other domains of the academic portfolio. In fact, trainees who take a leadership role in the creation and development of lecture series and courses may use their experience as evidence for leadership and management in their portfolios. **Figure 6.1** demonstrates the relationship between teaching and the other domains of the academic portfolio.

Figure 6.1 Relationship between teaching and other domains

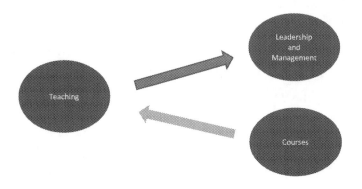

It is worth noting that the purpose of delivering effective teaching is not only to aim at scoring high in the Teaching domain. It is also a mandatory skill required for consultants and independent practitioners who will be responsible for delivering teaching and training for future undergraduate students and postgraduate trainees.

Summary

- Trainees are expected to demonstrate evidence of regular teaching commitments as well as evidence of validated feedback related to such commitments.

- Development and delivery of lecture series or establishing a course or a curriculum would undoubtedly result in achieving the maximum score in the Teaching domain.

- Involvement in teaching activities contributes significantly to the Leadership and Management domain of the academic portfolio.

CHAPTER 7

Leadership and Management

Leadership and management skills constitute a significant part of medical academic portfolios. This applies to leadership and management skills within or outside the medical and clinical fields. Interestingly, there is a remarkable overlap between achievements within this domain and those of other domains of the academic portfolio, such as Research and Publications; Audit and Quality Improvement; and Teaching.

The foregoing highlights the significance of this domain and also highlights the fact that achievements within other domains invariably contribute to the Leadership and Management domain.

This chapter describes the most efficient approach to improving the Leadership and Management domain of the academic portfolio. This chapter of the book is not designed to show trainees how to become effective leaders and managers; instead, it will give valuable tips aimed at improving leadership and management skills. Such skills will continue to develop and expand throughout the progression of a trainee's career.

What is expected of a trainee?

Trainees are expected to demonstrate that they have been involved in significant activities within or outside their medical and/or clinical fields highlighting their leadership, management, and teamwork skills. Prioritisation and organisational skills are of equal importance as well. Considering the insufficient clarity regarding the expectations of trainees in leadership and management roles, it is crucial to identify areas that would result in scoring high in this domain.

Most appropriate activities for a trainee to participate in

Trainees could demonstrate their leadership and management skills via the following activities:

- completing leadership and management skills courses and fellowships
- taking leadership roles in research projects
- taking leadership roles in audit and quality improvement projects
- taking leadership and organiser roles in developing regional and/or national teaching programmes and courses
- actively participating in national and/or international collaborative projects
- taking leadership and/or management roles related to healthcare provision, such as a

national executive role within the British Medical Association or a trainee representative role of a specialist medical society or college
- organising local and/or regional educational meetings, including mortality and morbidity meetings, and multidisciplinary team meetings

As mentioned above, criteria for achieving maximum scores in this domain are not as clear as with other domains. In order to achieve the maximum possible score, trainees are advised to complete at least one medical and management course and to seek a representative or leadership role for a national or an international society or committee.

What other domains are influenced by this domain?

As clarified above, taking leadership roles in research and in audit and quality improvement projects, as well as roles in various teaching activities, serves as valuable evidence of achieving competencies of this domain.

Moreover, attending leadership and management skills courses also significantly contributes to this domain. **Figure 7.1** demonstrates the relationship between Leadership and Management domain and other domains of the academic portfolio.

Figure 7.1 Relationship between Leadership and Management domain and other domains

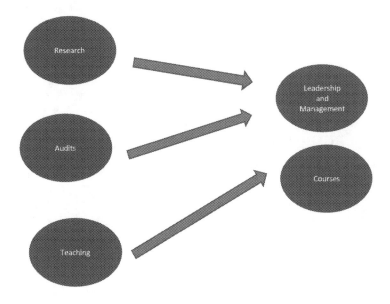

Summary

- The criteria for achieving a maximum score in the Leadership and Management domain are not as clear as with other domains. However, they remain achievable.

- Trainees could demonstrate their leadership and management skills through their engagement in different clinical and non-clinical activities.

- Trainees are advised to complete at least one medical and management course and to seek a representative or leadership role for a national and/or international society or committee.

CHAPTER 8

Prizes, Awards, Additional Qualifications

Winning an academic prize or award, or gaining an additional academic qualification, makes a significant positive impact on a trainee's academic portfolio. As most trainees do not have the opportunity to win a prize or award during the early stages of their training, such achievements would significantly enhance a trainee's portfolio. This chapter describes essential criteria required for a trainee to achieve a maximum score for such domains.

What is expected of a trainee?

Academic prizes and awards

In order to achieve the highest scores in this domain, trainees are expected to demonstrate that they have secured a **national prize** related to their medical field. The competition for such prizes or awards should have ideally been open to all medical undergraduates and/or postgraduates. In addition, high-achievement awards for primary medical qualifications such as

honours or **distinction**, which have been awarded to no more than the top 10 per cent of students, will also result in a high score in this domain.

Additional qualifications

In order to achieve the highest scores in this domain, trainees are expected to demonstrate that they have been awarded either **a PhD, or DPhil (Doctor of Philosophy)**—full-time research involving original work usually for at least three years' duration and ideally resulting in one or more peer-reviewed publications—or **an MD (Doctor of Medicine)**, a full-time research involving original work, usually for at least two years' duration and ideally resulting in one or more peer-reviewed publications.

It should be noted that other relevant single-year postgraduate courses, diplomas, and/or postgraduate certificates would also contribute positively to this domain.

How can a trainee achieve these domains?

As discussed earlier, some trainees will have been awarded additional qualifications prior to or during their studies for their primary medical degree. Some trainees take time out of training programmes at different stages of their training to gain and/or secure additional qualifications. Although securing an additional qualification is feasible and would have a significant positive impact on trainees' academic portfolios, it is well recognised that this domain might not be achieved in a timely manner.

It is worth noting that achieving an academic award or prize is not necessarily within a trainee's complete control. Engaging in more research projects, delivering more presentations, and achieving high scores in exams invariably increases the chance of being nominated for an award or prize.

Summary

- Authors recognise that most trainees might not have the opportunity to secure an additional qualification or win a prize or award during their training.

- It is understandable that some trainees will take time out of their training programmes at different stages of their training to seek and eventually secure additional qualifications.

- Securing an additional qualification is feasible and makes a significant positive impact on trainees' academic portfolios, although it is well recognised that this domain might not be achieved in a timely manner.

CHAPTER 9

Essential Nontechnical Skills

Training in medicine is undoubtedly tough. The content is challenging; expectations are high; and the length of both undergraduate and postgraduate education and training is comparably longer than that of any other profession. Such facts, with their associated financial, social, and health implications, need to be balanced carefully by the trainee so adequate resources may be deployed appropriately and expectations may be managed in a timely manner.

It is well recognised that medicine attracts highly competitive and motivated individuals. This remains the case from early undergraduate years through to postgraduate training. Consultants and independent practitioners are expected to prove they are up to date in relation to the latest guidelines, new training techniques, and innovations in their field. This constitutes an integral part of their professional development plan and appraisal processes.

It is also worth noting that the style of learning, teaching, and education in the field of medicine differs substantially from that of other fields. Undergraduate students and postgraduate trainees are expected to self-manage their training and education to a large extent, under the supervision and guidance of their seniors, supervisors, and tutors.

Despite available frameworks and approved curricula for different specialties, there is a fast-evolving expectation that students and trainees should take the lead on their education and training under close supervision of their supervisors. This is quite different from the old-style didactic teaching, which predominantly depended on feeding knowledge rather than delivering problem-based learning and promoting interactive knowledge gathering. Understanding such evolving challenges is of utmost importance to trainees and undergraduate medical students.

The following advice is crucial to doctors in training:

Do not panic

While this seems easier said than done, panicking over academic achievements is essentially counterproductive and serves only to exacerbate trainees' stress and anxiety. It is recognised that trainees are continuously under immense pressure to perform and achieve. This pressure usually starts in the early years of undergraduate education and continues throughout the postgraduate training years.

Panicking about lack of timely achievements will only exacerbate a trainee's concerns. There is always a fine line between being anxious about achieving and overstressing in relation to challenges. The sooner the balance is achieved, the better the outcome for doctors in training. It is recommended that trainees seek early advice from their trainers and mentors to ensure that any of the above challenges are highlighted and eventually tackled in a timely manner.

Get enough rest

Adequate rest and sleep is crucial to high performance. Clinicians who are overworked are more likely to make mistakes and would potentially under-achieve. A tired trainee who does not sleep well will undoubtedly underperform in all aspects of his or her career progression. Academic portfolio achievements are not an exception to this rule. In order to score high in your academic portfolio, you have to avoid factors leading to burnout and stress. Adequate breaks between long working shifts allows physical and mental recovery which would eventually lead to high performance.

Manage your time

Effective time management is crucial to doctors currently in training and further throughout their career progression. Avoid being in a situation where there is too much to do in a limited period of time. The amount of information and knowledge a trainee is expected to master is huge. Always remember that no trainee will be able to master every single aspect of the curriculum at early stages of his or her training.

The aim should always be to manage as much as practically possible within the limited time and with the limited resources available. Always note that time is a precious commodity that cannot be reclaimed when lost. Time management however is a skill that can be taught and mastered. Doctors in training are reminded that an issue that is currently important but not urgent will eventually be urgent if not dealt with in a timely manner.

Pay attention to other aspects of life

Always pay attention to other aspects of your life. It is obvious from the aforementioned discussion points that training and medical education are time-consuming. They make a significant impact on a trainee's social life and well-being. While this might sound like a basic advice, there is no doubt that even half an hour of daily exercise could potentially make a huge impact on trainees' resilience and ability to perform under pressure. Investment in health and well-being will eventually pay off several years down the line. Healthy practitioners are generally more productive than those with ill health. Doctors in training are encouraged to invest in quality time with their families and friends.

Seek advice

Doctors in training are always reminded that there are people around them who may be asked for advice. This advice can range from technical advice from senior colleagues to simple non-technical advice from friends and family members. It is worth noting that colleagues who might only be one year senior to a doctor in training can give invaluable career advice when consulted. By seeking such advice at an early stage, a trainee may easily avoid several mistakes that could happen a few years down the line and rectify any mistakes already made in a timely manner.

Summary

- Panicking about and stressing over lack of academic achievements is always counterproductive.

- Time management skills are crucial to medical students and doctors in training. Such skills can be taught and mastered in a timely manner.

- Doctors in training are encouraged to look after their health and manage their time efficiently at early stages of their training.

- Doctors in training are encouraged to seek early technical and non-technical advice from colleagues, friends, and family members.

CHAPTER 10

Choosing a Specialty

As described in the previous chapters of *How to Enhance Your Medical Academic Portfolio*, there are various ways of enhancing medical academic portfolios. In this chapter, we will be explaining various ways of effectively choosing a specialty as a future career. It is thought that without being able to choose an appropriate specialty, the enhancement of medical academic portfolios for doctors in training would be irrelevant if the wrong specialty was eventually chosen.

One of the toughest decisions a trainee is expected to make at an early stage of his or her training is to choose a specialty. It is understandable that making a relatively early decision about a specialty of choice might not be possible for various reasons, some of which could not be influenced by the trainee.

A trainee should, however, be able to decide at an early stage whether he or she would want to pursue a career in a technically demanding specialty such as surgery, compared to an office or a lab-based specialty such as pathology. This broad choice could be readily made by the end of foundation training years.

Many factors should be taken into consideration when deciding about a specialty. This includes risk of burnout as well as life-work balance. Whichever specialty a trainee chooses, he or she should recognise that the choice will make a significant impact on his or her future at both the career and personal levels.

What are the factors to be considered while choosing a specialty?

Relationship and interaction with patients

Interaction with patients and their relatives is an integral part of clinical practice. Doctors in training are able to broadly understand their future career aspirations and ambitions during their late undergraduate and early postgraduate years. Such broad understanding would eventually help trainees achieve their future aspirations without unnecessary delays and hurdles. It is generally advised that if candidates are not passionate about interaction with patients and their relatives, then they should readily consider a specialty associated with minimal interaction and is more office based or lab focused.

Life-work balance

It has long been traditional to call this "work-life balance"; however, the authors of this book are strongly in favour of reversing the order and calling it "life-work balance". It is crucial to recognise the importance of getting this balance right at an early stage. An overworked clinician will not be able to give his or her best to patients, potentially reducing the chances of reaching his or her full career potential. It has always been perceived that surgical specialties provide poor life-work experience and are associated with a high level of burnout and stress. This situation has significantly improved in the last few years, and there has been an evolution of some surgical specialties with high job satisfaction and improved life-work balance.

Technical and procedural ability

If a junior doctor in training is not keen on performing technical procedures or does not have the tactile dexterity to perform certain tasks, then surgical specialties in general might not be the best choice. Medical specialties and subspecialties, on the other hand, should never be perceived as specialties devoid of procedural skills and technicalities. Certain medical specialties have evolved over the last few years with the introduction of various technical skills, including endoscopy/colonoscopy within the gastroenterology sub-specialty and bronchoscopy within the context of respiratory medicine. It is all about finding the right balance between the requirement of the specialty and the ability of the clinician to perform certain tasks and exercise certain skills.

Willingness to pursue a certain specialty for life

Doctors in training are encouraged to find at early stages, whether or not they can see themselves practising within a certain specialty for the rest of their professional lives. They are encouraged to consider various options and constraints of such specialities during training and throughout their independent practice. If they conclude that they would not be able to pursue their professional career within their proposed specialty, they are strongly advised to find an alternative specialty or different work pattern including less than full time employment.

What is a systematic approach to choosing a specialty?

Areas of scientific or clinical interest

As a general rule, if a trainee has been fascinated by pharmacology and physiology at the undergraduate level, then he or she could consider anaesthetics as a specialty of choice. On the other hand, if a trainee has been fascinated by anatomy and tissue dissection, then he or she could potentially consider surgery and various surgical subspecialties for their postgraduate training. Also if brain sciences were areas of interest, then neurology and neurosurgery could be the best way forward. These are broad general rules and can be applied flexibly based on individual preferences, available training opportunities as well as other associated limitations.

Direct versus indirect patient care

If a trainee is interested in direct patient care and close patient interaction, then medical and surgical specialties would be suitable as a future career. If the trainee, however, is more interested in specialties where direct patient interaction is not prevalent, then radiology and pathology may be sensible choices.

Intensity of interaction with patients

Specialties such as internal medicine, psychiatry, and general practice are associated with prolonged patient-clinician interaction as compared to surgical specialties, where the interaction might be more intense but occur over a shorter period of time. Interventional radiology is one of those specialties where there is intense but short lived patient-clinician interaction during certain short-lived interventional episodes. Trainees should be aware of the above facts and such factors need to be taken into consideration when choosing a specialty.

Fatigue and burnout

As previously stated, stress levels and chances of burnout are generally major deciding factors when choosing a specialty. Many factors could potentially contribute to high stress levels and burnout, including the level of bureaucracy and administrative workload related to a particular specialty. As a general rule, the longer and more unsocial the hours of work, the higher chance of fatigue and burnout. It is recognised that the level of support provided to individual clinicians from their wider teams is also a major contributory factor to burnout and fatigue. Dynamics within various organisations and institutional cultures also play a major role in aggravating or relieving stress and burnout.

Patients' outcomes

The decision about a specialty could also be influenced by patients' outcomes. Those individual clinicians who are highly driven by and focused on favourable patients' outcomes should think twice prior to choosing a specialty where patients' outcomes are generally less favourable. While there have been significant advances in various specialties' outcomes, we all recognise that specialties such as palliative medicine, neurology, and oncological neurosurgery are generally associated with less favourable outcomes where focus could mainly be directed towards symptom control rather than disease cure.

Personal skills and limitations

Trainees applying for a certain specialty need to ask themselves various questions. Are they good at laboratory-based tasks? Are they fascinated with teaching theoretical medicine at the university level? What about technical and communication skills? Are they good communicators? How competitive are they?

The above factors and associated queries should be taken into consideration before choosing a specialty, especially for those specialties which are highly sought-after. Doctors in training are reminded that early planning is crucial to success.

Financial gains and salary incentives

Clinicians do not enter the medical field aiming at financial gains. In fact, if the trainee uses his or her communication and technical skills in business and/or production industry, he or she will potentially achieve more financial gains in that field as compared to the field of medicine. Medicine is practised predominantly because of the passion and dedication of medical practitioners. Financial security, however, remains important for successful and sustainable career progression. Trainees are encouraged to ensure that the projected income of the chosen specialty will potentially cover their cost of living for years to come.

Finally, following the foregoing discussion points, if the trainee remains unsure about a specialty of choice, then he or she should consider shadowing senior colleagues for a short period of time. Shadowing senior colleagues in various specialties can provide invaluable experience and information in relation to how to choose certain specialties. The decision made following a short period of shadowing will eventually be based on real-life experience.

Summary

- Do not rush your decision. Take your time, and consider limitations as well as time and resource constraints.

- Know your strengths and potential weaknesses while deciding on your specialty of interest. Make sure though, that you decide in a timely manner.

- Choosing a specialty depends on several factors, including personal abilities, fields of interest and trainees communication skills.

- Seek early advice, shadow seniors if necessary, and always consider life-work balance.

CHAPTER 11

Challenges to Achieving a Highly Competitive Academic Profile

There are many challenges that doctors in training could potentially face in relation to achieving a highly competitive academic profile. Such challenges might include financial challenges, health and well-being challenges, time constraints, and unexpected service disruptions. These are only a few examples; the list goes on.

Some of the aforementioned challenges will be addressed in further detail in this chapter of *How to Enhance Your Medical Academic Portfolio.* It is expected that the majority of challenges can be dealt with efficiently as long as guidance is sought from supervisors and mentors in a timely manner. There remain situations where medical students and doctors in training may face certain unexpected challenges that are not under their control and cannot be overcome in a timely manner. In such circumstances, a clear plan and a potential exit strategy should be created far in advance.

Financial challenges

It is well recognised that studying medicine is costly. Taking a break from direct clinical practice to conduct a focused academic or a lab-based research project could have a significant impact on trainees' income. It is recognised that hospital-based clinical jobs generally generate more income compared to lab-based non-clinical jobs. This is partly because such clinical posts usually attract banding/extra payment for on-call and out-of-hours activities.

If a doctor in training decides to pursue a research-based non-clinical career for a short period of time, then taking on ad hoc on-call clinical commitments would not only reduce the associated financial burden but would also allow doctors in training to keep their clinical, technical and communication skills up to date while working in a non-clinical setting. Such an approach is highly recommended by the authors of this book.

Health challenges

Life is never short of surprises and good health must not be taken for granted. A minor health issue that leads to a six-month absence can make a significant negative impact on achieving the academic competencies required for a competitive academic portfolio.

As stated earlier in this book, maintaining a healthy lifestyle is crucial to a trainee's performance in all aspects. There are, however, circumstances that cannot be either influenced or controlled by doctors in training, especially emergencies and unexpected adverse health issues. The majority of such circumstances as mentioned earlier can be neither predicted nor controlled.

The role of each doctor in training is to invest as much as he or she can, while enjoying good health in preparation for any unexpected circumstances. *How to Enhance Your Medical Academic Portfolio* aims at highlighting such circumstances far in advance in order for trainees to be well prepared for such unexpected but potentially disrupting eventualities.

Time constraints

As stated earlier, time is a precious commodity. Doctors in training need to be aware of time constraints from the outset. Academic activities and associated projects need to be planned in such a way that these may be achieved realistically and in a timely manner without affecting other clinically focused activities.

It is the authors' recommendation that doctors in their early years of training should not get involved in more than two academic research projects at once. This will ensure that doctors involved in such projects remain focused on deliverable and achievable targets.

When doctors in training reach a certain level of seniority, they may then start getting involved in several projects in a leading/supervising capacity. Prioritisation is also a skill that is crucial to enhancing academic portfolios. It is essential for doctors in training to be able to prioritise academic commitments during the early stages of their training. This will ensure maximisation of academic achievements within the available limited time and resource constraints.

Unexpected service disruptions

Doctors in training should recognise that clinical services may be disrupted for various reasons. This might potentially have a significant impact on trainees' abilities to achieve their academic competencies in various clinical settings in a timely manner.

Expecting and being prepared for unexpected service disruptions in the early stages of training potentially mitigates such risks. Unplanned service disruptions may be caused by several factors, some of which are understandably not within the control of doctors in training. Examples include the following:

Pandemic disruptions

It has been clearly witnessed that the 2020 Covid-19

pandemic has had a detrimental effect on clinical services with associated worldwide service disruptions. Many patient wards, clinical areas, and intensive care units across the world have been overwhelmed with Covid-19 patients throughout 2020 and beyond. This has resulted in several cancellations of elective activities on a scale that has never been witnessed before in recent history. It is well recognised that elective activities provide invaluable data for research projects. Such reduced elective activities will eventually make a negative impact on certain data available for academic research projects. On the other hand, emergency admissions and those admissions related to Covid-19 sepsis may invariably enhance the availability of academic data related to such an illness and its associated pathogenesis for several years to come. Such data could be used to conduct and generate a large number of academic projects that would eventually enhance trainees' academic portfolios.

Doctors in training are encouraged to grab every opportunity available for enhancing their academic portfolios, whether within their specialty or within other, interdependent specialties. This principal applies to emergency as well as elective activities.

Service relocations

Service relocation and centralisation occurs continuously in the NHS and equivalent health systems. Such services move across sites and even across regions in an attempt to provide the best service to patients and their families. Centralisation of cancer services at tertiary referral centres is a clear example of such relocations that eventually resulted in better patients' outcomes.

With the relocation of certain services, doctors in training should expect that they will need to be flexible, pragmatic, and adaptive to such changes. Doctors in training are also expected to be able to collect data from different sites, irrespective of whether they physically work at such sites or not, as long as they protect and secure patients' confidentiality and follow data protection rules and regulations.

With new advanced methods of connectivity through online apps and virtual meetings, doctors in training are now, more than ever before, able to connect with various colleagues, exchanging thoughts and research methodologies, sharing data securely, and using technology to its full potential. Such enhanced connectivity also enabled clinicians and doctors in training to attend educational and multi-disciplinary meetings at certain hospital sites even if such sites no longer provide certain services.

Trainees' relocation

Training in medicine and surgery evolved over many years. Doctors in training used to stay in the same region or even with the same group of hospitals throughout the entirety of their postgraduate training. Nowadays, relocation to different regions or even to different countries is common and is actually encouraged. This invariably could enhance and consolidate trainees' technical skills, knowledge, and experience at both clinical and non-clinical levels.

Doctors in training are encouraged to be prepared to mobilise, relocate, and plan their academic activities based on the aforementioned potential events. While relocation can be looked at as a major challenge, it is worth noting that doctors in training could utilise the aforementioned challenges to their benefit by looking at enriching their academic portfolios when they move around during the relocation periods. Such relocations could potentially enable doctors in training to widen their expertise and explore practices and techniques that are not readily available within their local regions.

Setting unachievable goals

One of the biggest challenges a trainee can face is setting himself or herself up to fail by opting for unrealistic or unachievable goals. There is a fine line between ambitious goals and unrealistic ones. Enthusiasm and ambition are major drivers for improvement and progression; however, unrealistic targets are generally set to fail from the outset—and will make a negative impact on career progression.

When a portfolio is evaluated, three completed projects are by far more favourable than six partially finished ones. This applies to audits, research projects, postgraduate degrees, and quality improvement projects. The ability to complete projects is a major indicator of time management skills and strategic planning, both of which are considered crucial skills for doctors in training.

Doctors in training are advised to recognise, at an early stage, any unfinished or potentially delayed projects and set a timescale for eventual completion. If, for whatever reason, a timely completion is not possible, then an exit strategy should be determined to avoid wasting invaluable resources that would negatively impact on a trainee's career progression.

Lack of focus

Doctors in training are encouraged to remain focused throughout their training. Lack of focus may be caused by various factors, stress being one of these. Lack of focus or clear vision is considered one of the challenges that doctors in training might face during their training. Being focused allows doctors in training to determine their aim and the means to achieve their career goals by way of the shortest route.

Other factors that can affect focus are ill health, hormonal disturbances, sleep deprivation, and pressure from peers, seniors, and supervisors. It is recognised that some of these factors might not be under the trainee's complete control. Others, however, can be influenced or at least altered if recognised early. The role of mentors and supervisors in determining and tackling such challenges remains crucial.

Summary

- There are various challenges for doctors in training who aspire to achieve a highly competitive academic profile.

- Financial and health challenges, as well as unexpected service disruptions, remain among the most common challenges.

- Trainees are advised to consider some challenges as opportunities to grab and invest in. They are reminded that determination and focus are crucial to success.

Throughout the various chapters of *How to Enhance Your Medical Academic Portfolio*, several ways of enhancing the academic portfolios of medical students and doctors in training were highlighted and clearly identified. This book also highlighted factors that could affect the ability of individuals to achieve highly competitive academic profiles. In the following closing paragraphs, we will highlight the impact of achieving highly competitive academic profiles on patients' care and clinical outcomes.

It is crucial to view strong academic achievements as a means to an end, the end being to achieve better patient care, reduce mortalities and morbidities, and improve the quality of patients' lives. The majority of academic activities for clinicians and clinical scientists are based on the desire to provide analyses, explanations, and evidence for any patient care-related activity. Such academic drive will eventually provide much needed information that will invariably guide the trainee in clinical practice. Evidence-based medicine (EBM) aims at integrating the best available research outcomes with technical and clinical expertise. EBM has made great gains in popularity since the late 1990s and is continuing to reshape the future of our clinical practice.

Practising evidence-based medicine is an evolving process of continuous learning and self-improvement. Patients' care continuously creates a need for obtaining valuable information about clinical presentations, diagnostics, and decision-making. It is recognised that the best available evidence continuously evolves and that what is best for today's practice could potentially change in the near future.

EBM derives its core information from research and other related academic activities provided by clinicians, clinical scientists, and laboratory-based researchers. By being academically active from the early years of training, medical students and doctors in training will undoubtedly be able to develop and maintain a mindset that will enable the creation and provision of essential clinical evidence. Such evidence is required for improving patient care and enhancing patient experience.

Involvement in academic activities from the early stages will eventually promote analytical and critical thinking. It will also enhance accuracy and precision of diagnostic skills and the ability to take correct timely decisions. It is crucially important that healthcare professionals are able to develop essential key skills required for their clinical practice, including the ability to critically appraise scientific information and analyse data as well as the ability to incorporate and utilise such evidence in clinical practice.

Involvement in various academic activities enhances the ability to identify problems, analyse potential causes for such problems, and create a strategy for resolution. Being able to start a project and finish on time is also a clear indicator of the ability of researchers and academic candidates to manage time and work under pressure. Such skills are crucial during the years of independent practice as consultants and qualified general practitioners.

This now brings *How to Enhance Your Medical Academic Portfolio* to a conclusion. It was a genuine attempt by the authors to create a concise document and a path that will lead doctors in training to understand the various ways by which they may enhance their academic portfolios. Doctors in training are encouraged to look at this book as a means to an end, with the end being to create a competitive portfolio. It is worth noting that the advice and methodology given in this book can be applied to all practitioners who would like to pursue an academically fulfilling career, even after completion of their training.

Independent practitioners who are academically active will eventually witness the impact of such activities and achievements on the outcomes of their patients. The authors also believe that those independent practitioners who are academically focused are more likely to use evidence-based medicine and analytical thinking when looking after their patients and also when training their junior colleagues. This will eventually lead to better and improved outcomes.

As stated earlier in this book, academic achievements in clinical practice should be mainly focused on improving clinical outcomes. There is nothing less fulfilling than spending precious time and valuable resources on projects that will potentially end up on a shelf in a library. The best reward for a clinician is a piece of research or academic achievement that results in a better clinical outcome or a better quality of life for a patient or group of patients. Authors of this book highly recommend that doctors and clinicians in training should mainly focus on research projects that are clinically relevant.

We wish all success to readers of this book in pursuing an academically fulfilling career and in enhancing their academic portfolios for years to come.

Moustafa Mansour
Surgical Excellence Clinic Limited

Shahab and Shahin Hajibandeh

Printed in the United States
by Baker & Taylor Publisher Services